MORE CLASSICAL TAB

Cherry Lane Music Company
Director of Publications/Project Editor: Mark Phillips
Manager of Publications: Gabrielle Fastman

ISBN-13: 978-1-57560-927-0
ISBN-10: 1-57560-927-4

Visit our website at www.cherrylane.com

CONTENTS

6	Allegretto	*Carulli*
8	Allegretto (from Northern Dances)	*Giuliani*
3	Andante	*Carulli*
10	Andante Cantabile	*Tchaikovsky*
12	Arabian Dance (from *The Nutcracker*)	*Tchaikovsky*
20	Ase's Death (from *Peer Gynt*)	*Grieg*
17	Ave Verum Corpus	*Mozart*
22	Bist du bei mir (You Are with Me)	*Bach*
24	Bourree (from *Partita in C*)	*Anonymous*
26	Cancion O Tocata	*de Murcia*
28	Caro mio ben	*Giordani*
30	Dedicatoria (from *Stories of Youth*)	*Granados*
32	Eine Kleine Nachtmusik, Second Movement	*Mozart*
34	Espanoleta	*Sanz*
36	Evening Prayer (from *Hansel and Gretel*)	*Humperdinck*
38	Gerbe des Fleurs	*Ferrer*
40	Intermezzo (from *Cavalleria rusticana*)	*Mascagni*
42	Lagrima	*Tarrega*
44	Minuet in G	*Bach*
46	Panis Angelicus (O Lord Most Holy)	*Mozart*
48	Pie Jesu (from Requiem)	*Fauré*
51	Rondeau	*Mouret*
52	Sinfonia	*Bach*
54	Sleepers, Awake	*Bach*
56	Sonata in A	*Scarlatti*
60	Study in D	*Giuliani*
61	Study in D	*Sor*
64	Study in D Minor	*Carcassi*
70	Symphony No. 3, Third Movement	*Brahms*
66	Symphony No. 5, Second Movement	*Schubert*
68	Symphony No. 9, Second Movement	*Dvořák*

Andante

By Fernando Carulli

Moderately slow

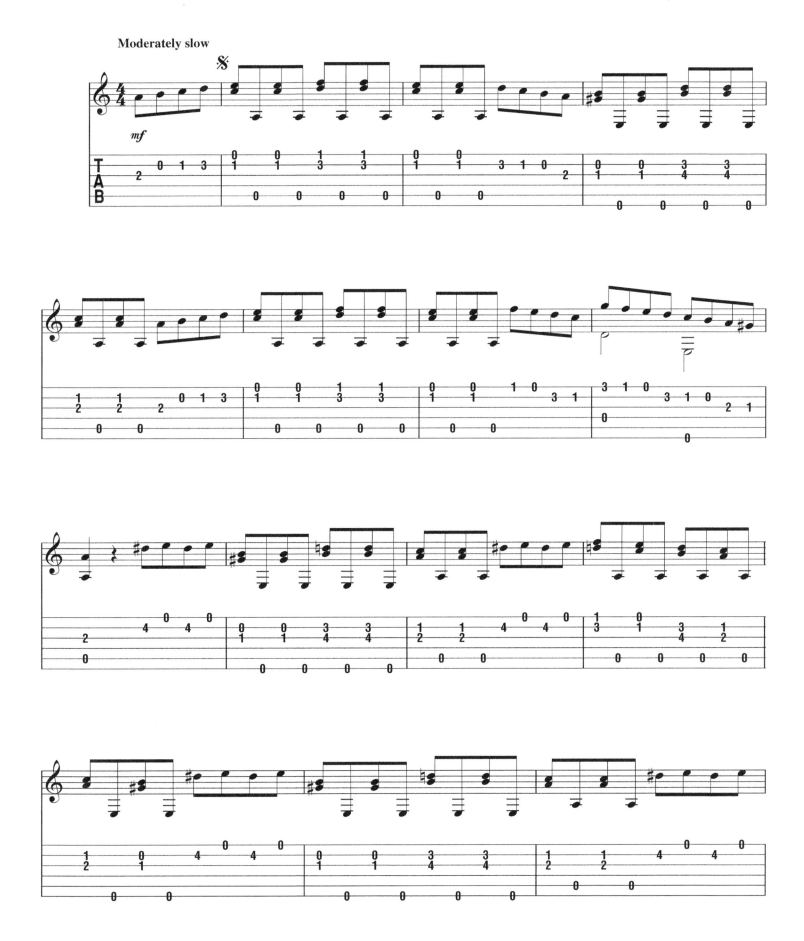

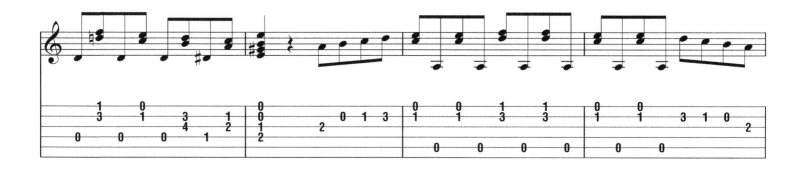

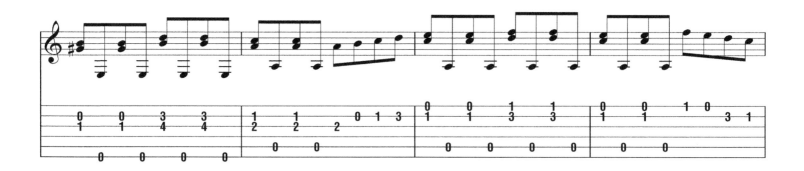

Fine

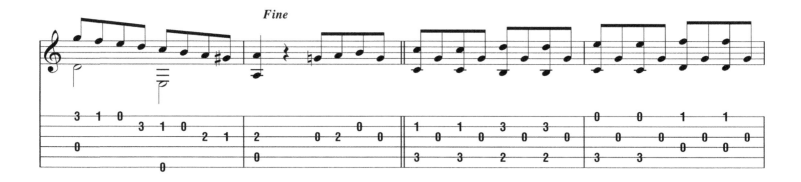

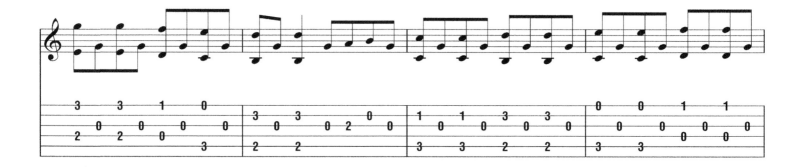

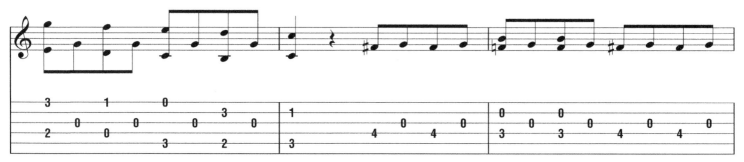

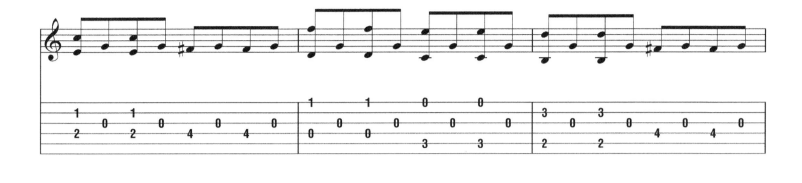

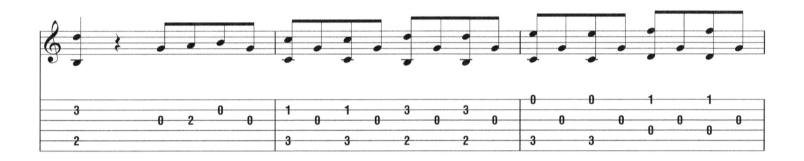

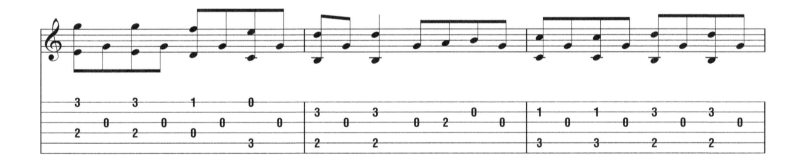

D.S. al Fine

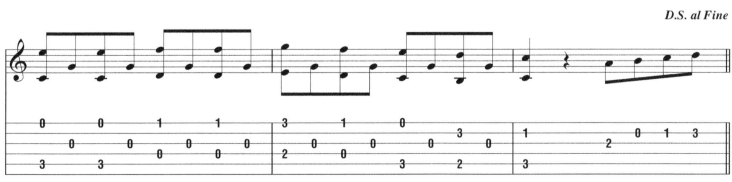

Allegretto

By Fernando Carulli

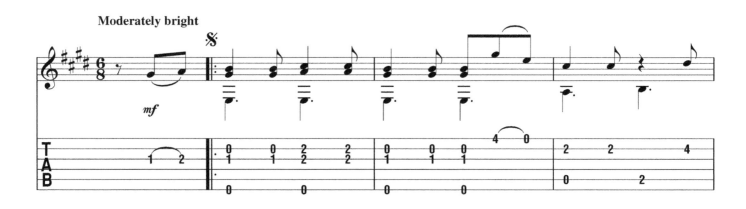

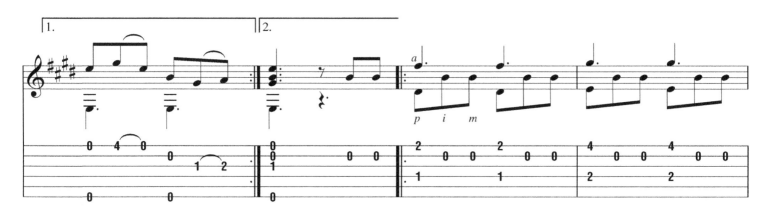

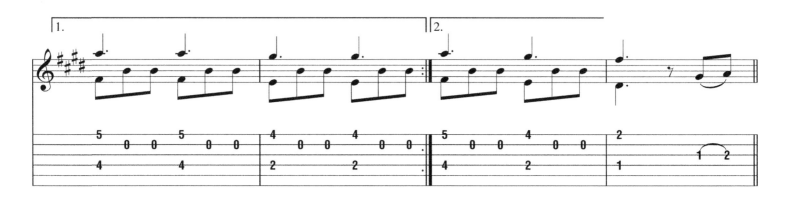

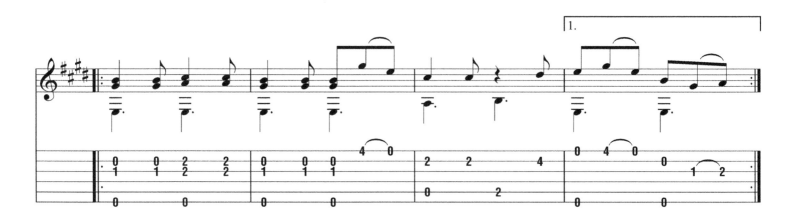

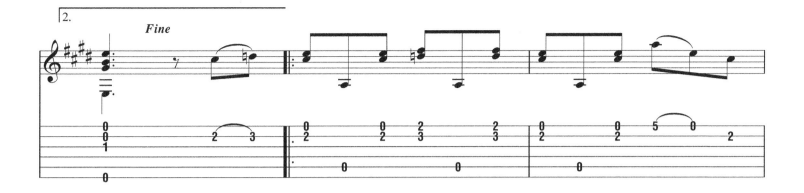

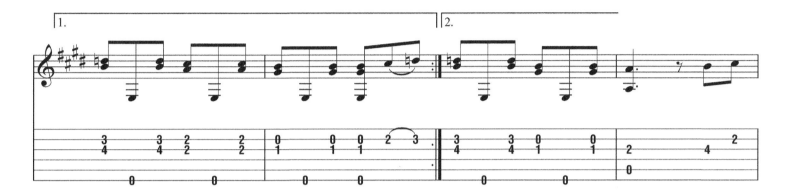

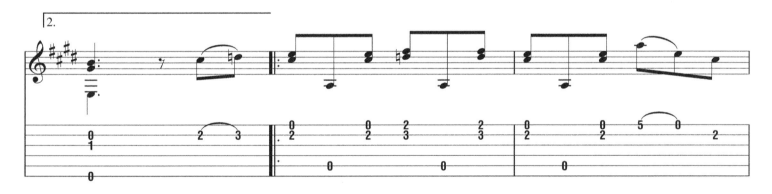

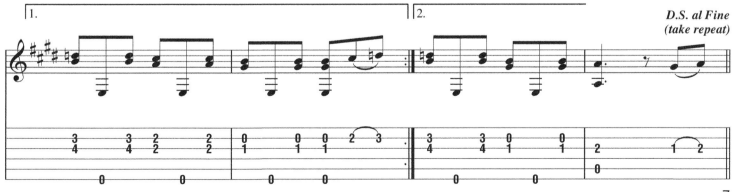

Allegretto

from Northern Dances

By Mauro Giuliani

Moderately bright, in 2

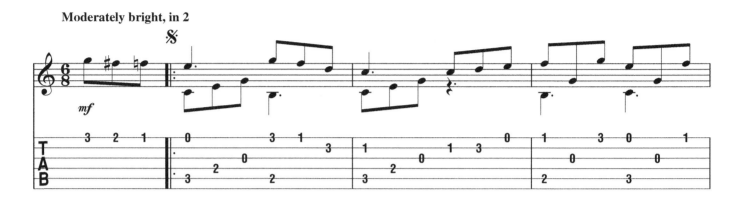

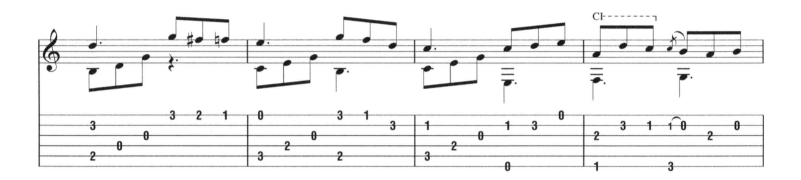

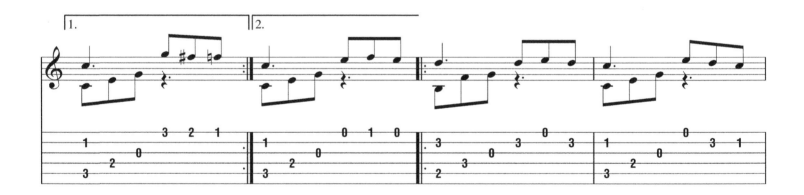

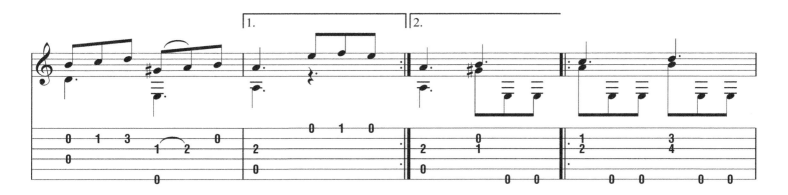

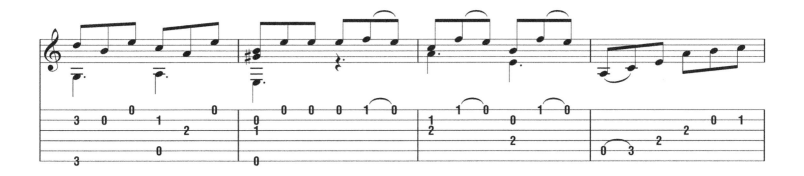

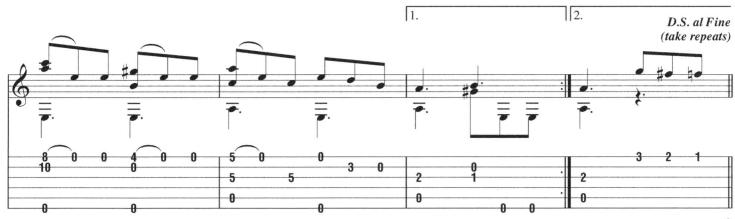

Andante Cantabile

from 5th Symphony

By Peter Il'yich Tchaikovsky

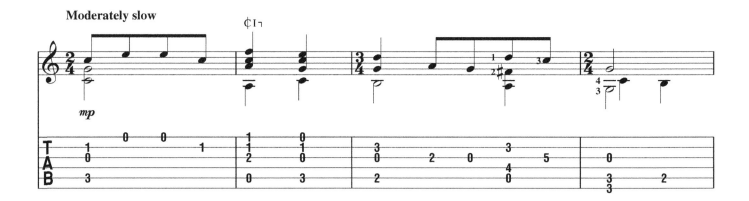

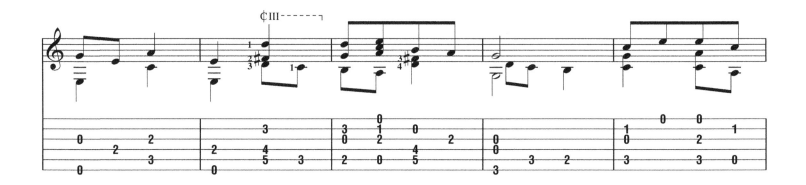

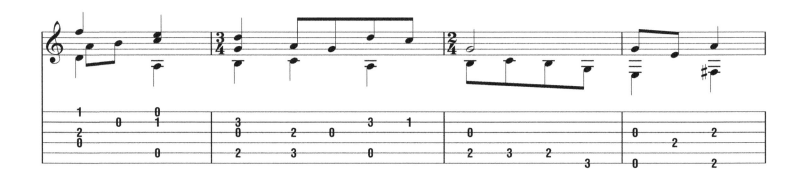

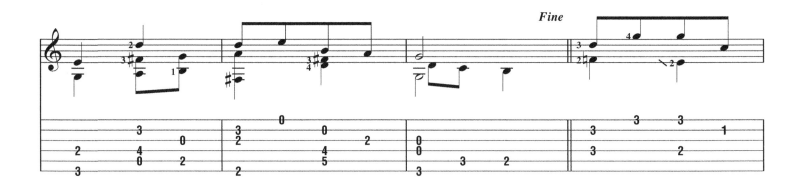

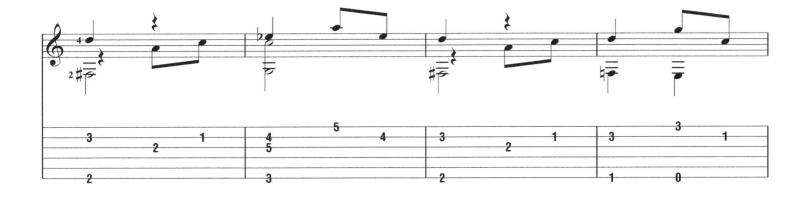

D.C. al Fine

Arabian Dance
("Coffee")
from The Nutcracker

By Pyotr Il'yich Tchaikovsky

Tuning:
(low to high) E-B-E-G-B-E

Moderately fast

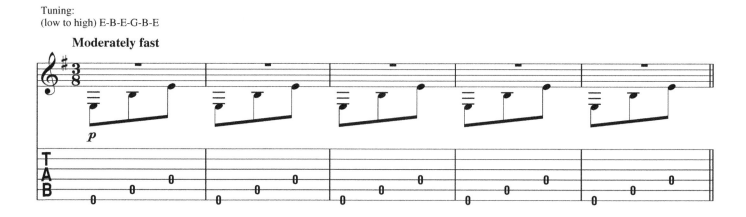

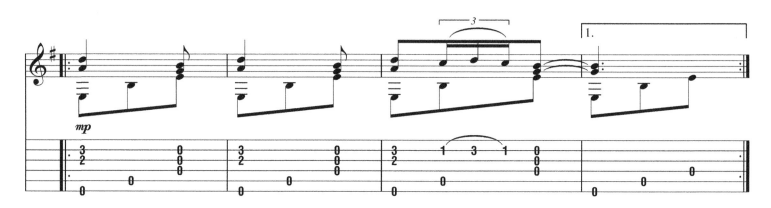

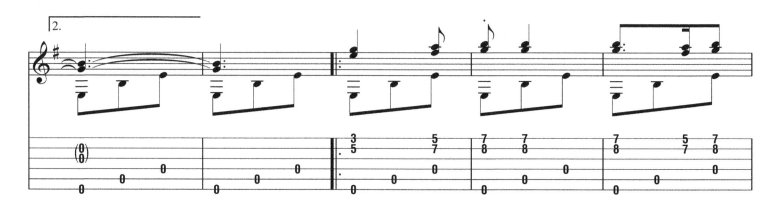

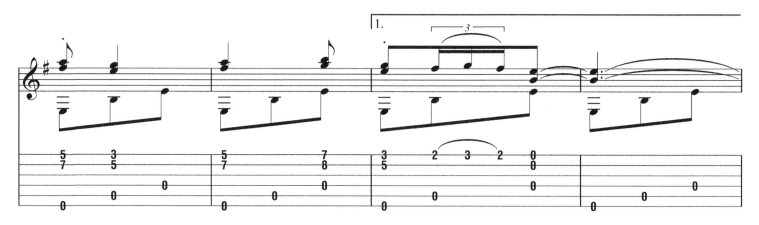

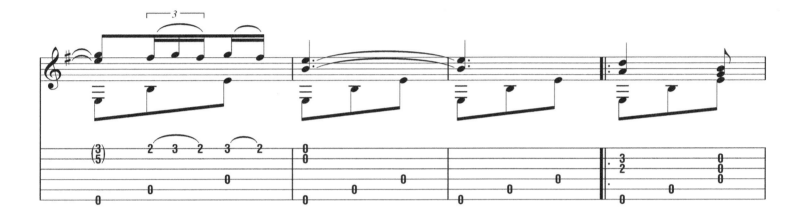

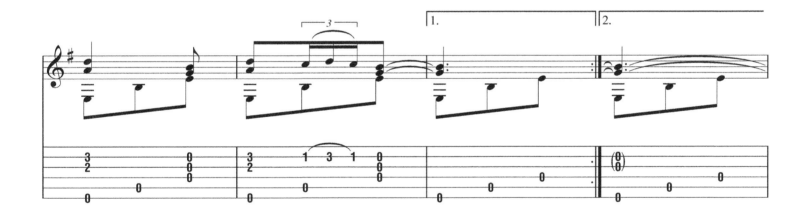

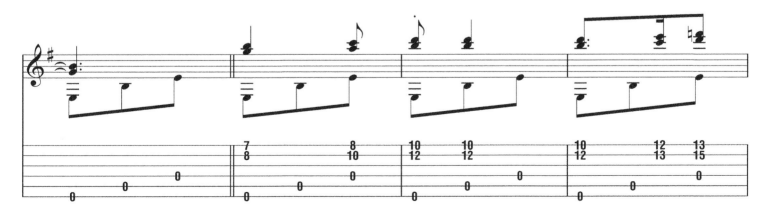

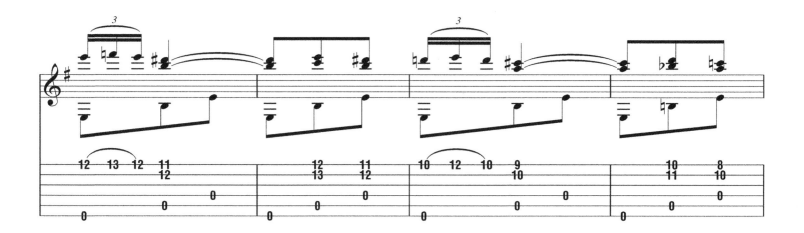

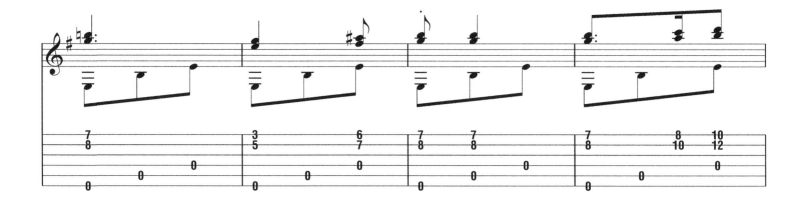

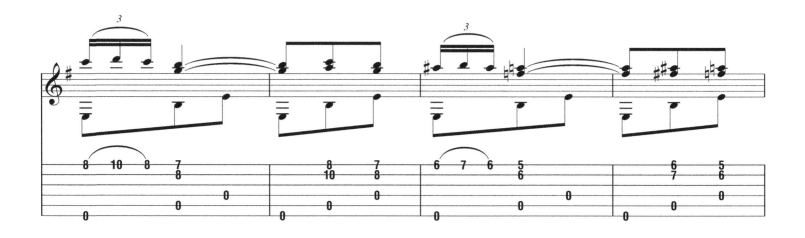

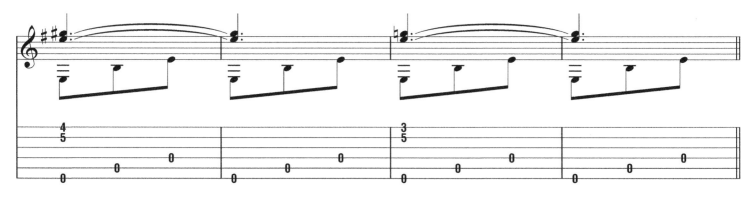

14

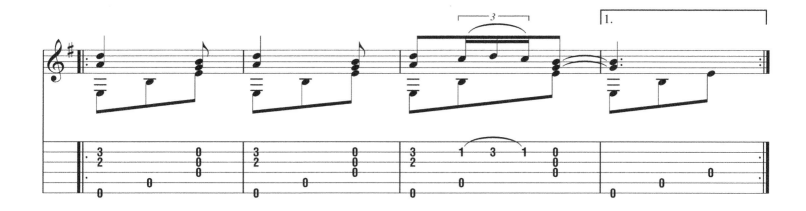

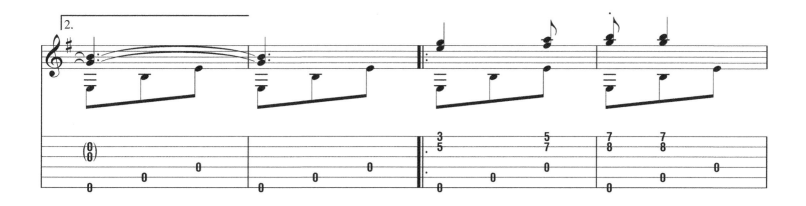

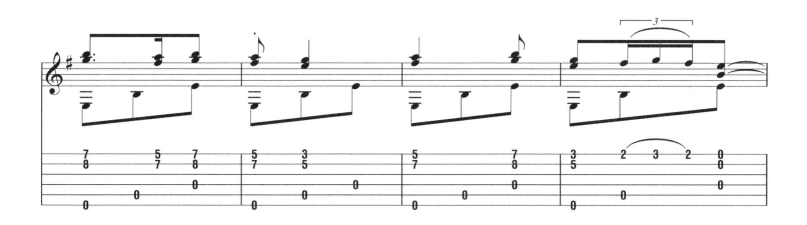

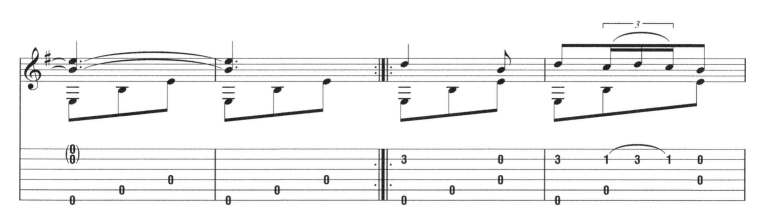

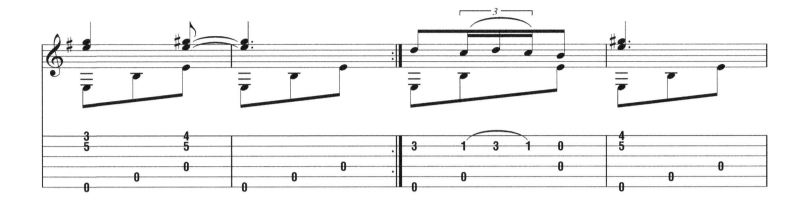

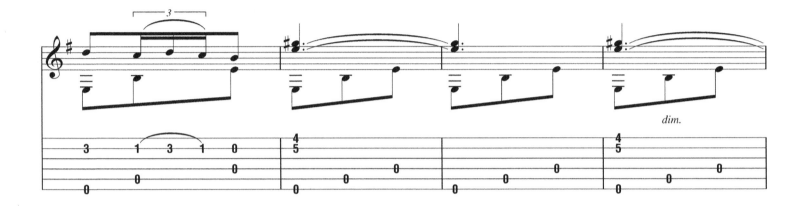

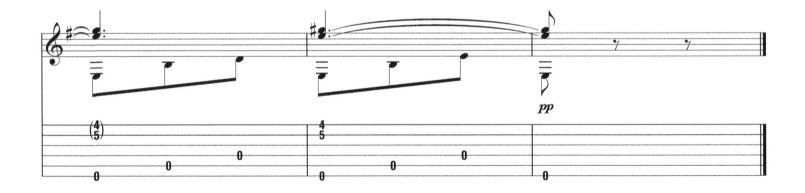

Ave Verum Corpus

By Wolfgang Amadeus Mozart

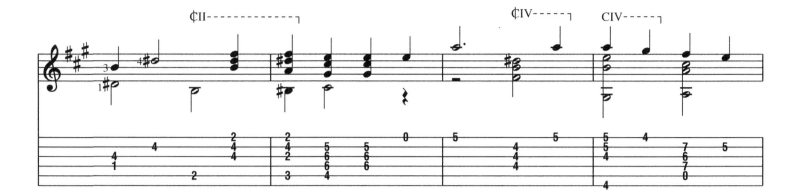

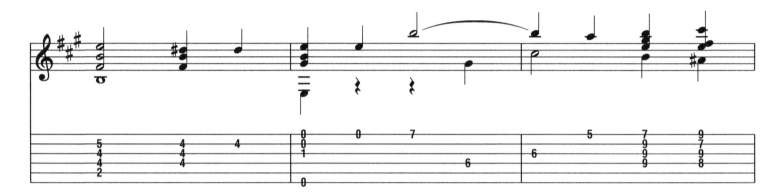

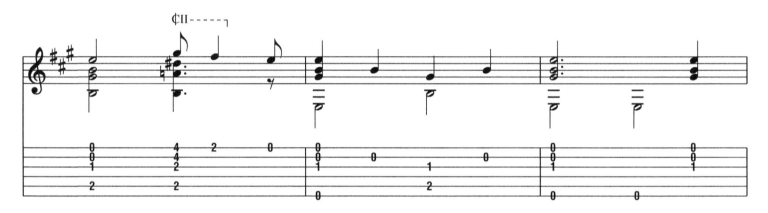

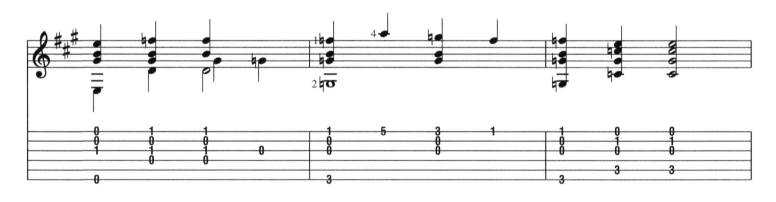

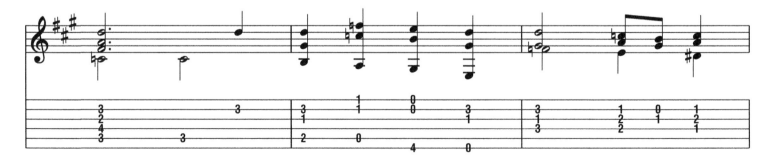

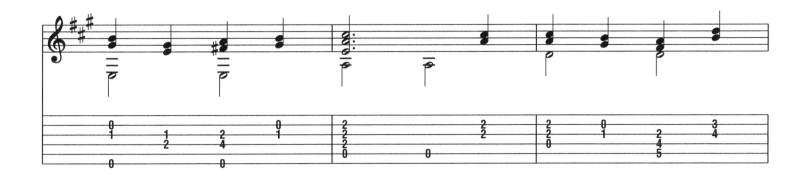

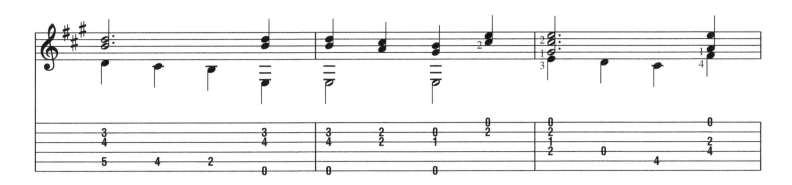

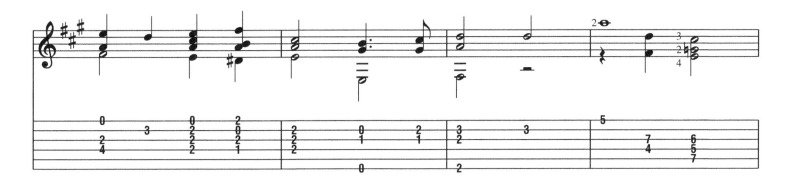

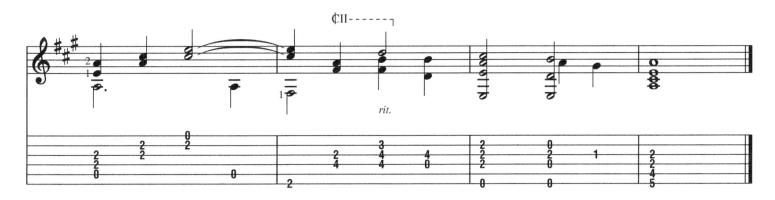

Ase's Death

from Peer Gynt

By Edvard Grieg

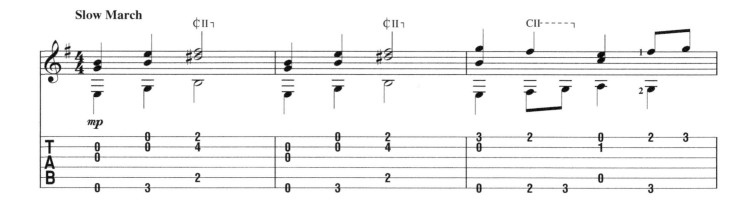

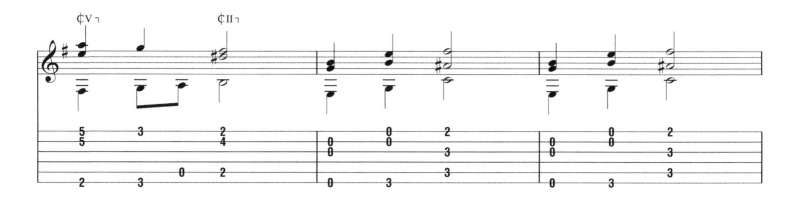

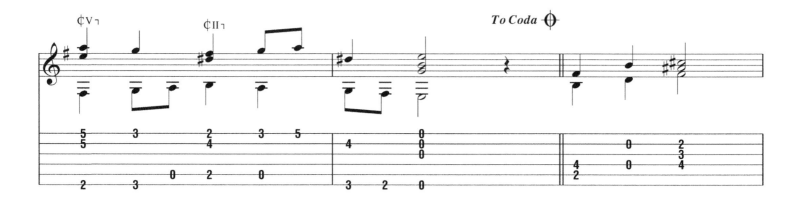

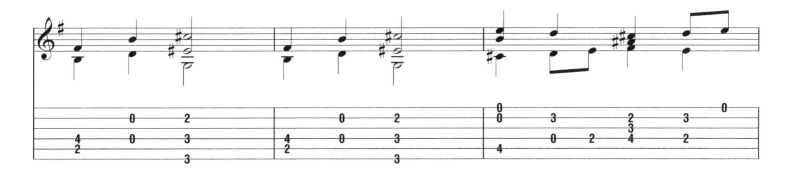

D.C. al Coda

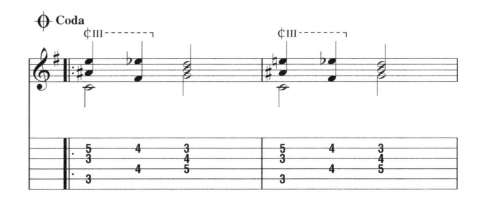

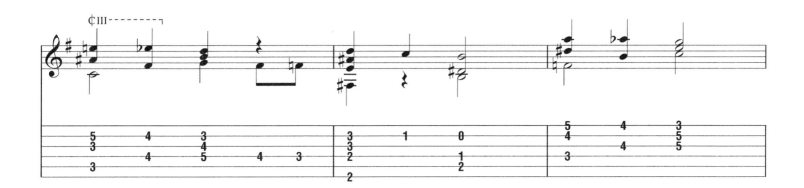

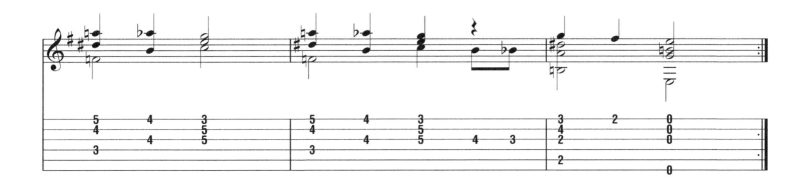

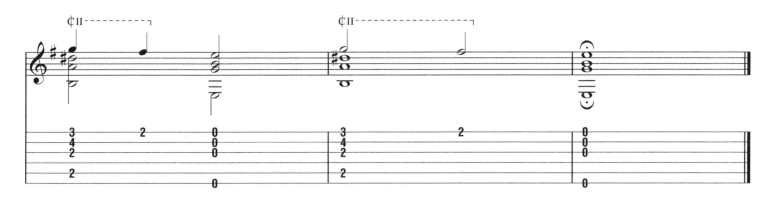

Bist du bei mir

(You Are with Me)

By Johann Sebastian Bach

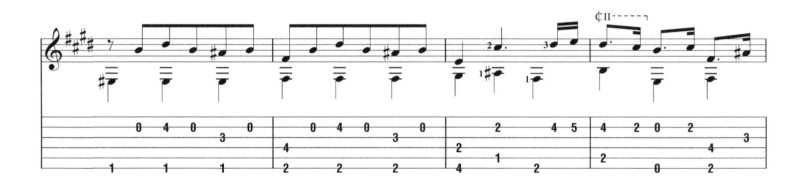

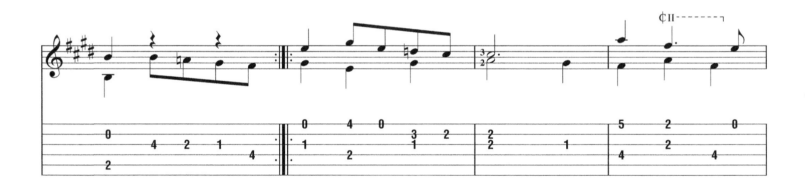

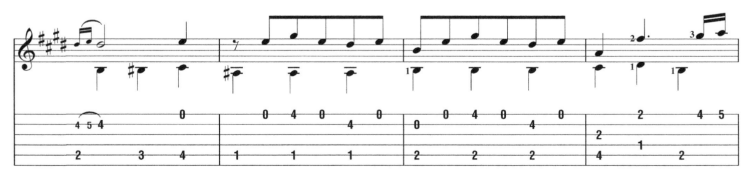

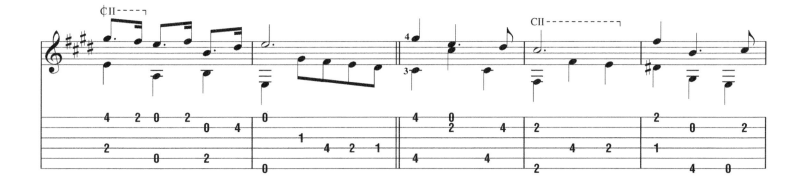

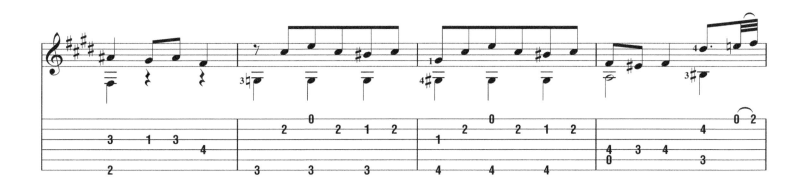

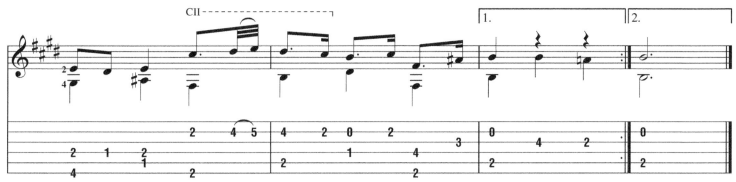

Bourree

from Partita In C

Anonymous

Moderately, in 2

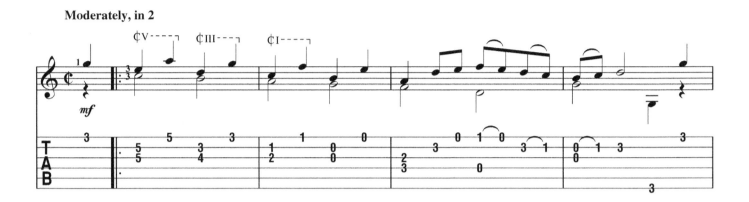

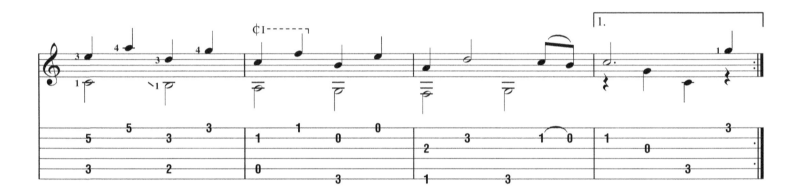

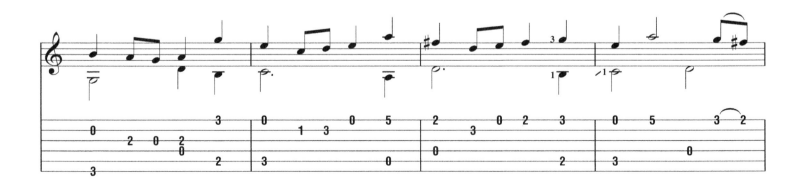

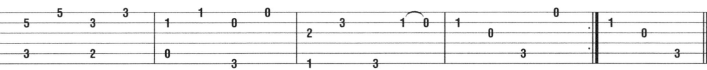

Cancion O Tocata

By Santiago de Murcia

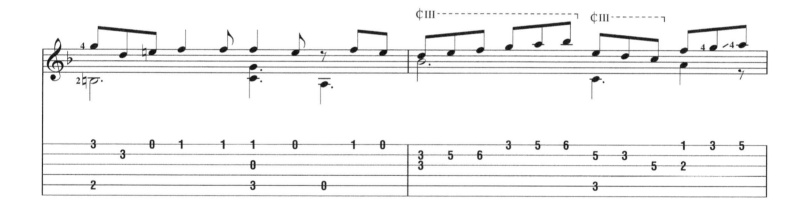

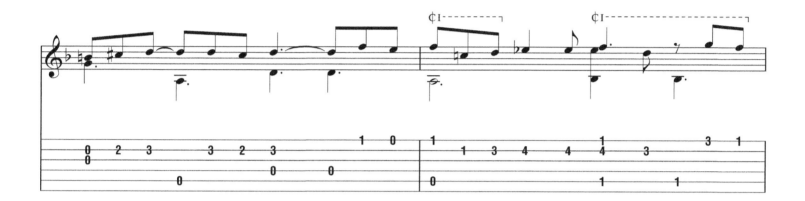

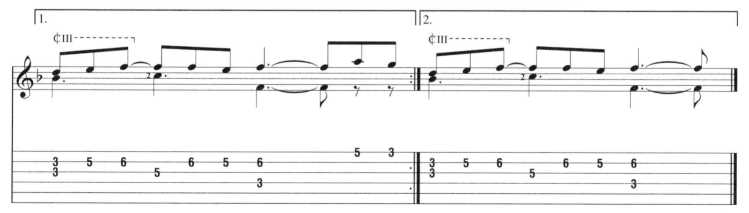

Caro mio ben

By Tommaso Giordani

Dedicatoria

from Stories of Youth

By Enrique Granados

Tuning: ⑥= D

Moderately slow

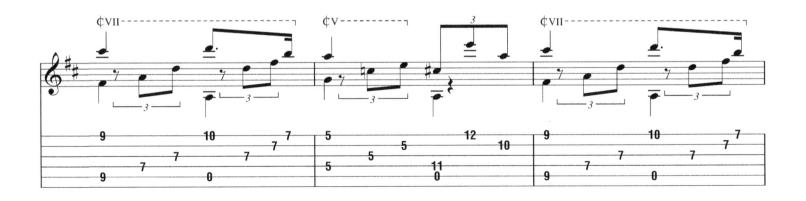

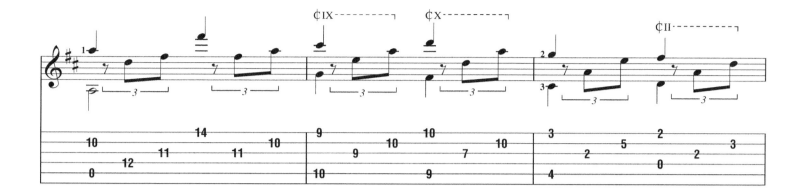

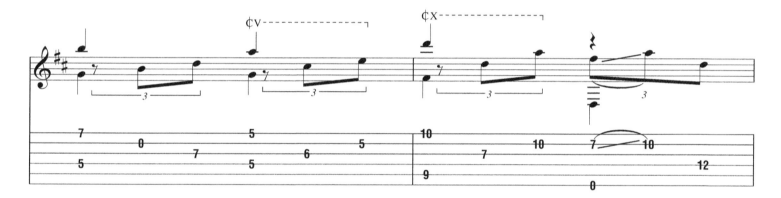

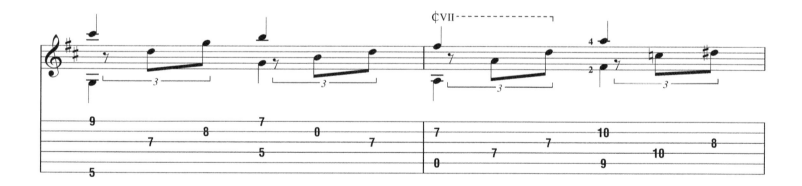

Eine Kleine Nachtmusik
("Romance")
Second Movement

By Wolfgang Amadeus Mozart

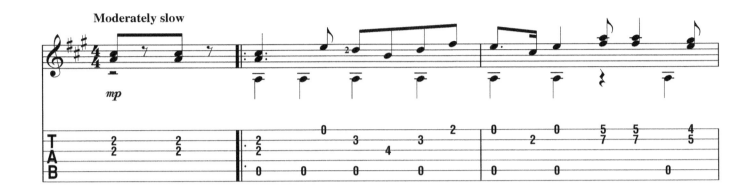

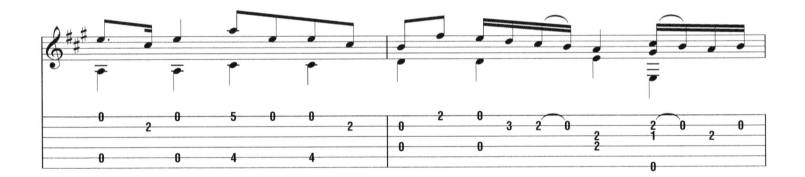

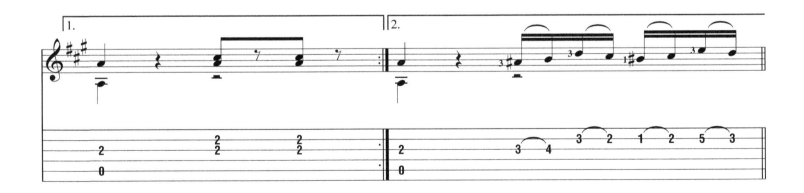

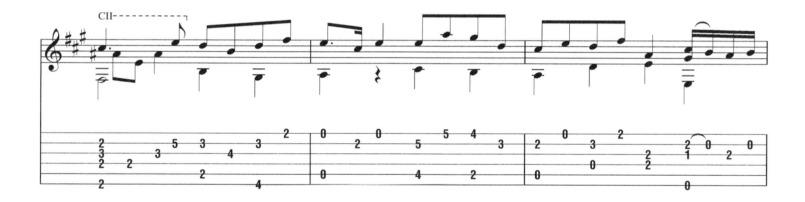

Espanoleta

By Gaspar Sanz

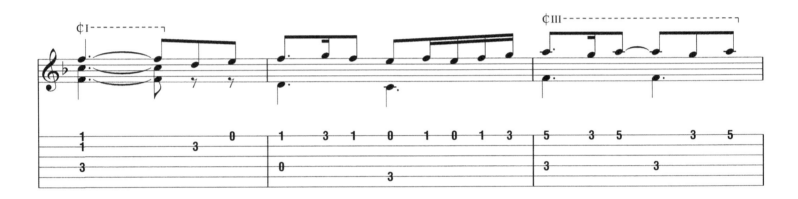

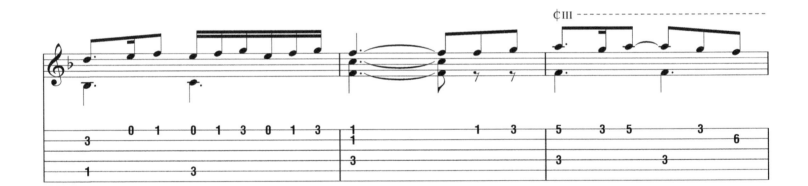

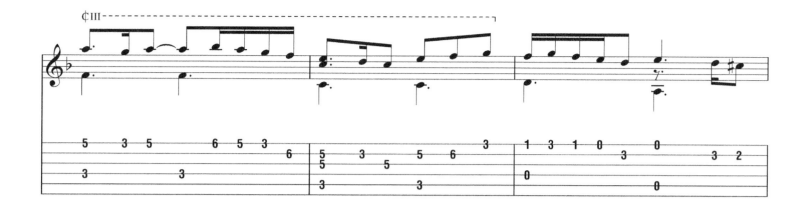

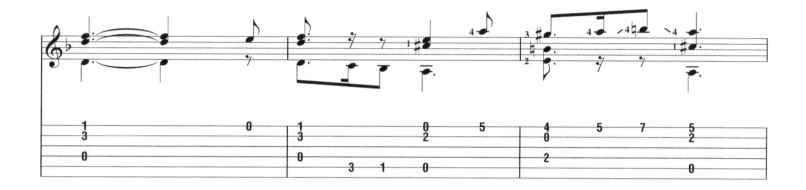

Evening Prayer

from Hansel and Gretel

By Engelbert Humperdinck

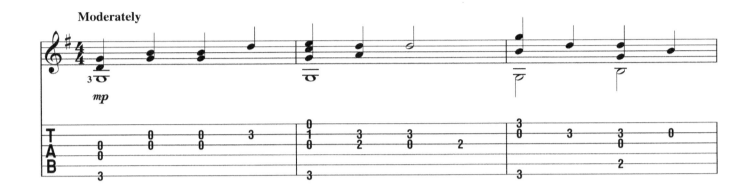

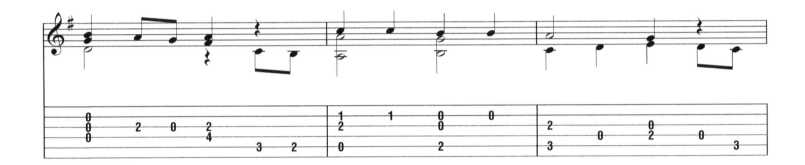

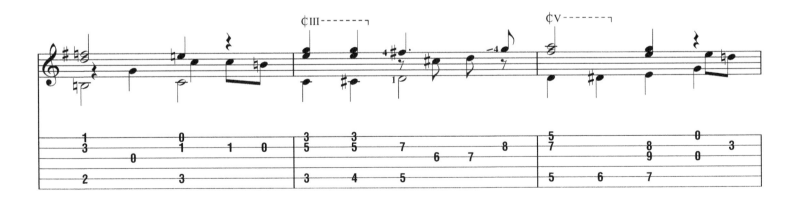

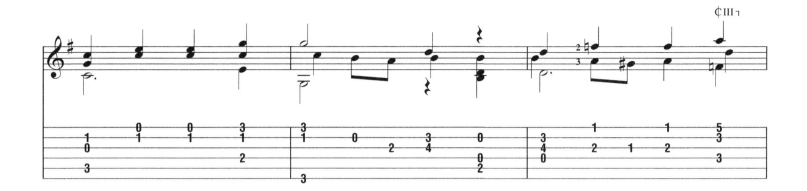

Gerbe des Fleurs

By Jose Ferrer

D.S. al Fine
(take 2nd ending)

Intermezzo

from Cavalleria rusticana

By Pietro Mascagni

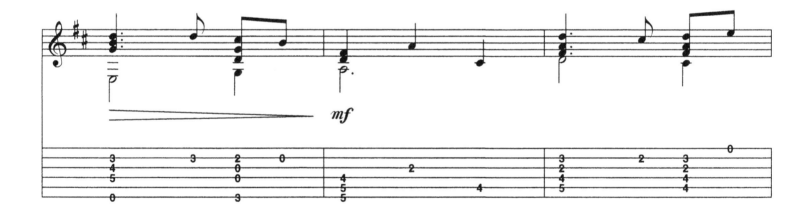

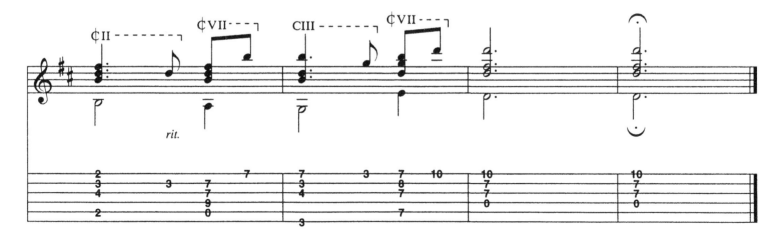

Lagrima

By Francisco Tarrega

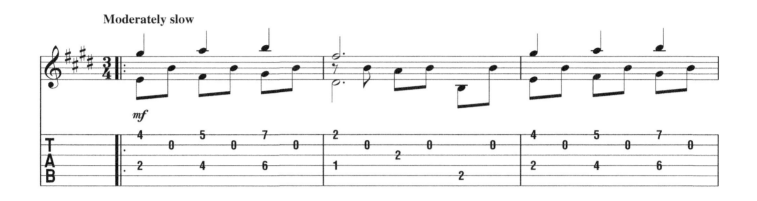

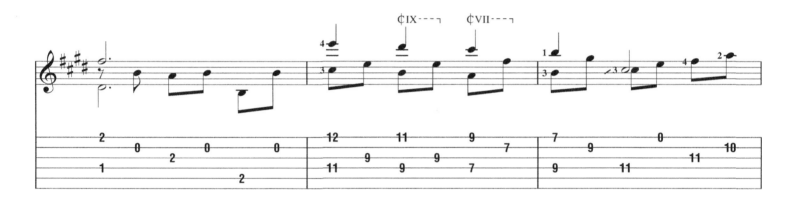

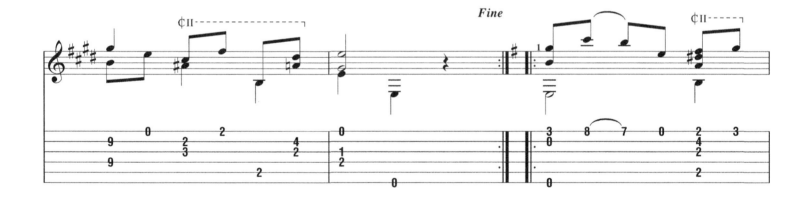

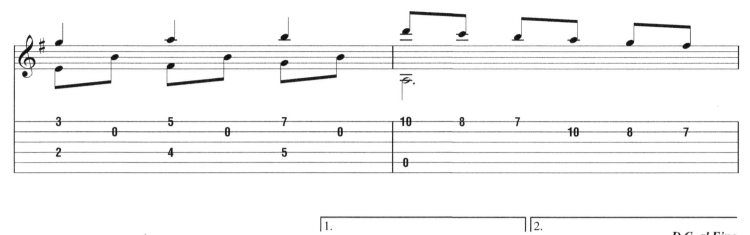

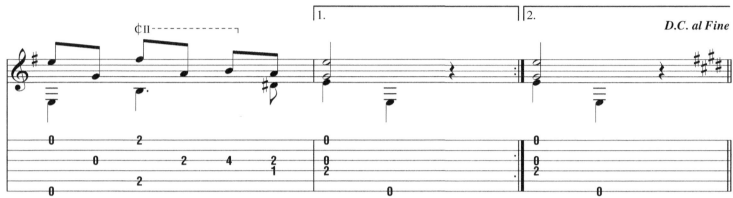

Minuet in G

from the Anna Magdalena Notebook (originally for keyboard)

By Johann Sebastian Bach

Moderately fast

mf

Panis Angelicus
(O Lord Most Holy)

By Cesar Franck

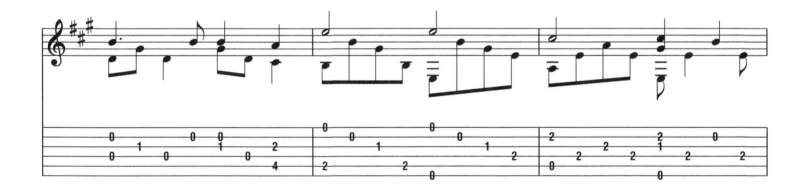

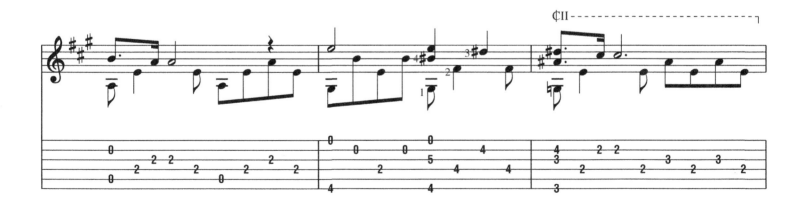

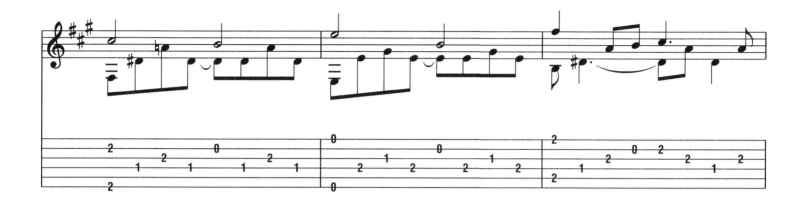

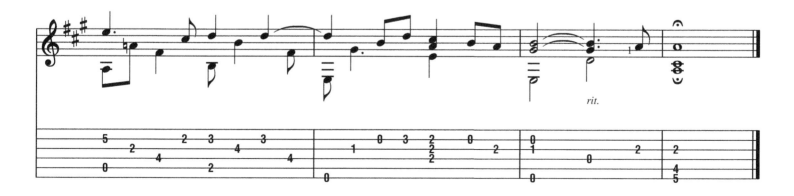

Pie Jesu

from Requiem

By Gabriel Fauré

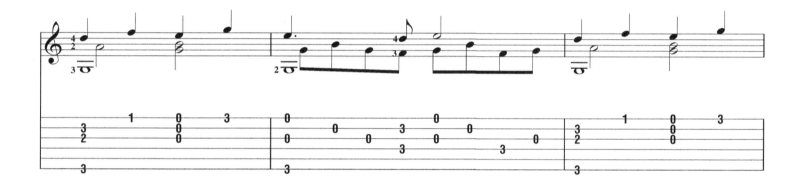

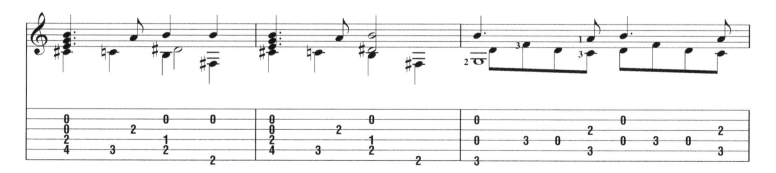

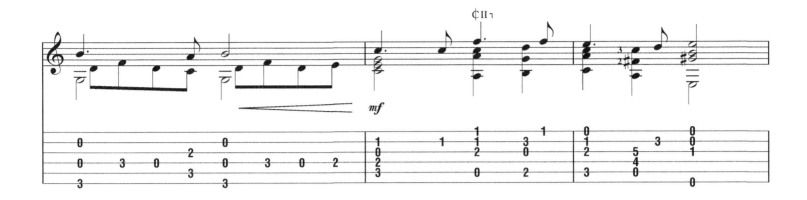

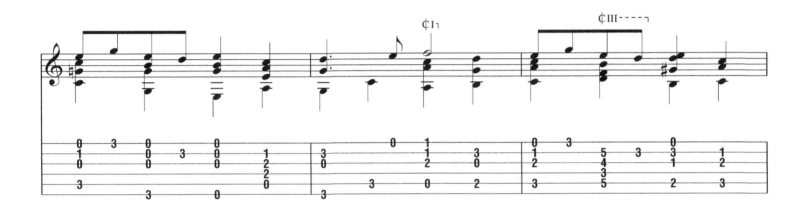

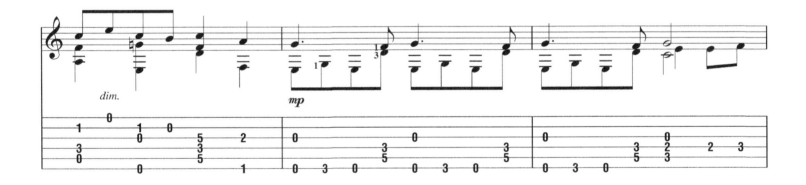

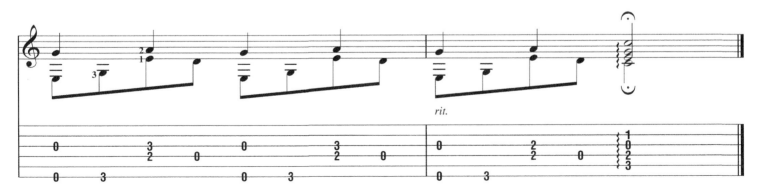

Rondeau

By Jean-Joseph Mouret

Moderately, in 2

Sinfonia

from Christmas Oratorio

By Johann Sebastian Bach

Moderately

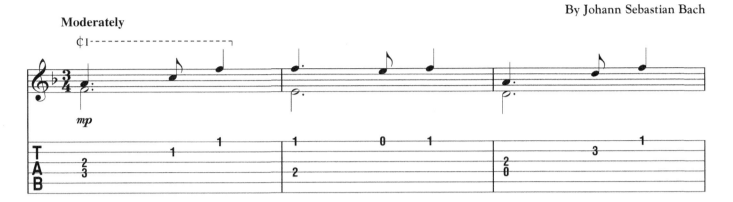

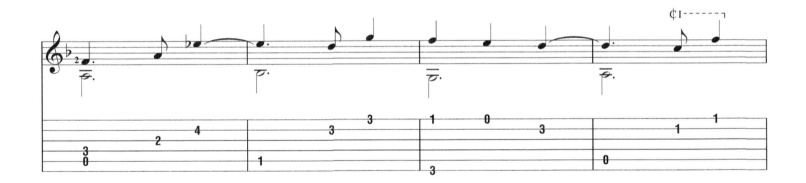

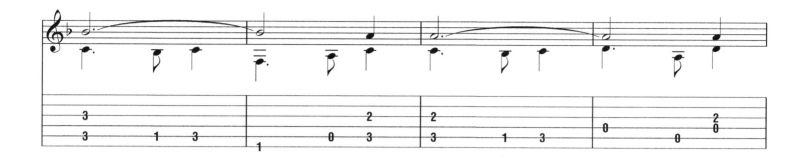

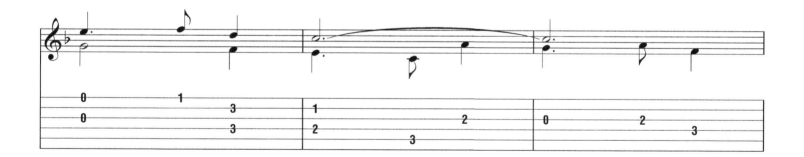

Sleepers, Awake
(Wachet Auf)
from Cantata No. 140

By Johann Sebastian Bach

Moderately slow, in 2

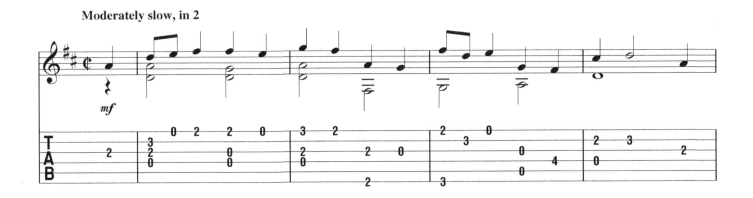

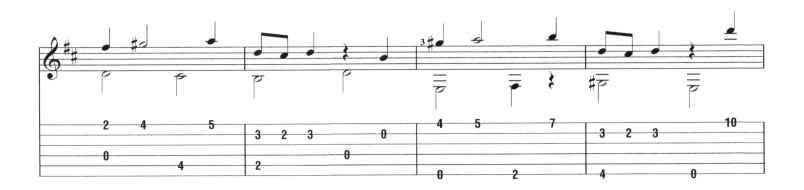

Sonata in A

By Domenico Scarlatti

Moderately slow, in 2

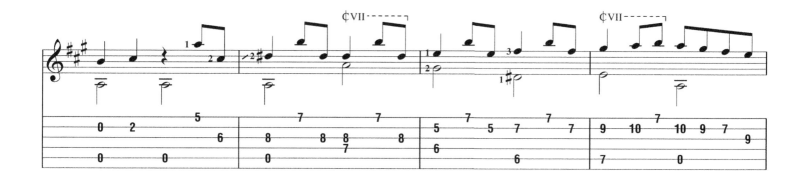

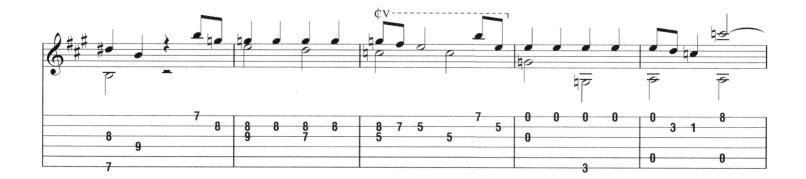

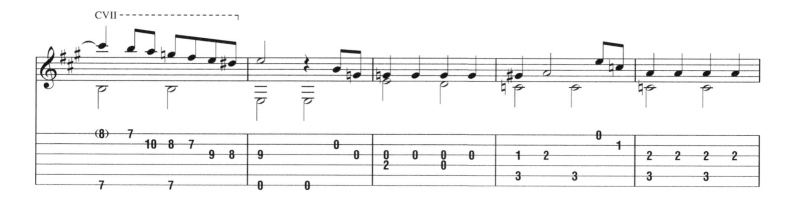

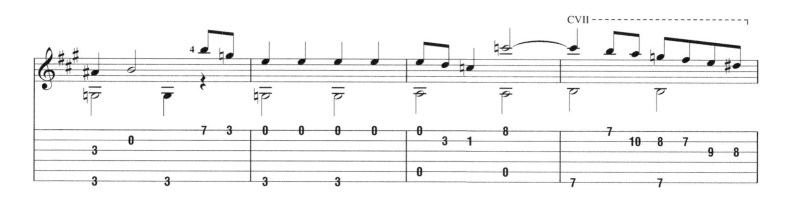

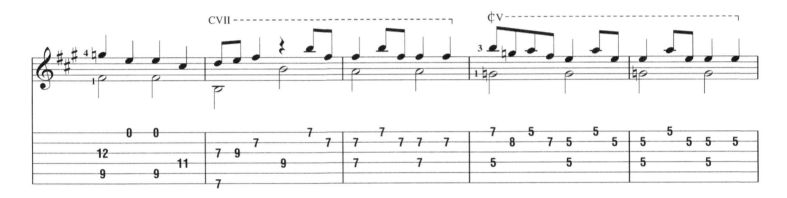

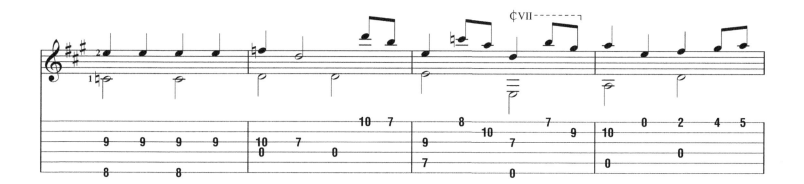

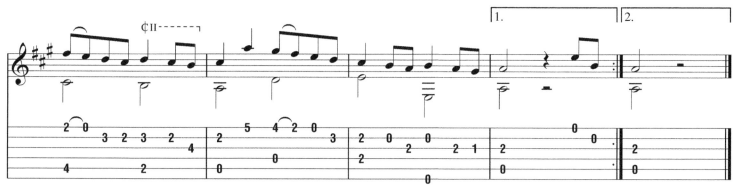

Study in D

By Mauro Giuliani

Moderately slow

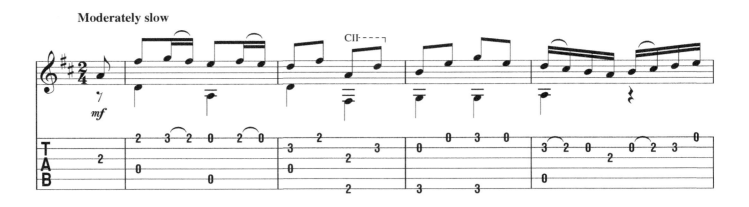

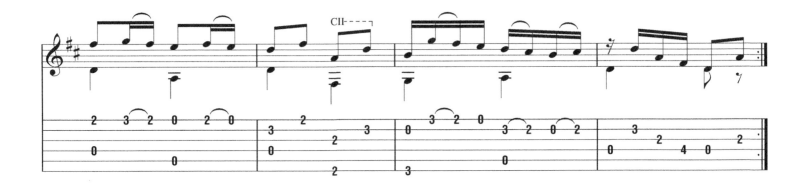

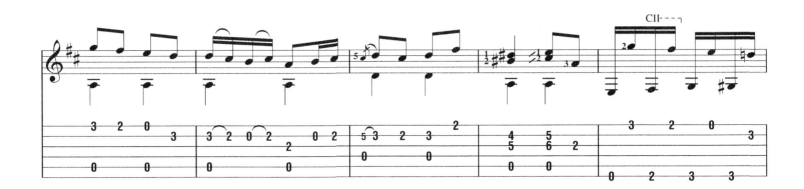

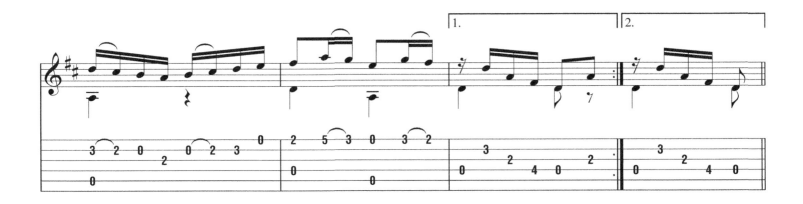

Study in D

By Fernando Sor

Tuning: ⑥ = D

Moderately bright

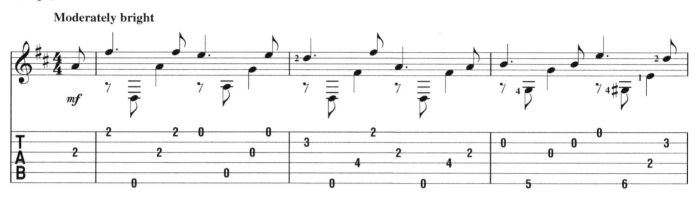

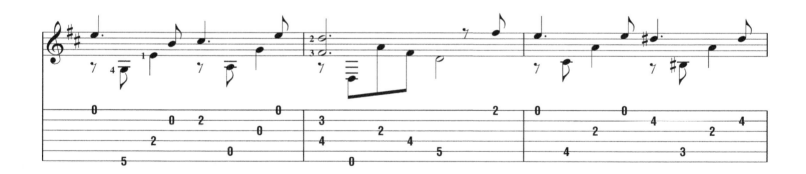

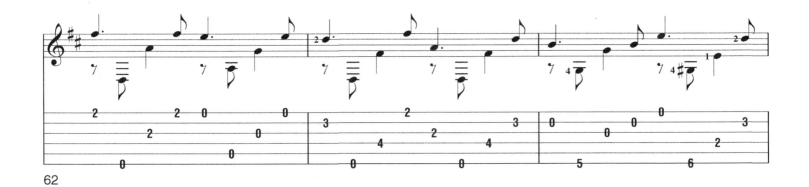

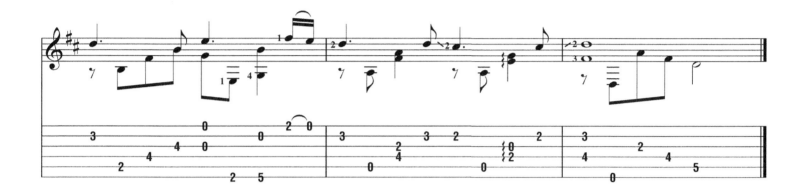

Study in D Minor

By Matteo Carcassi

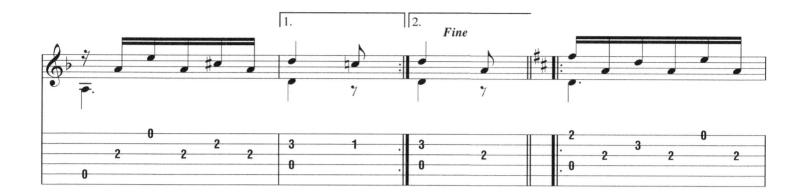

Symphony No. 5

from ANDANTE

By Franz Schubert

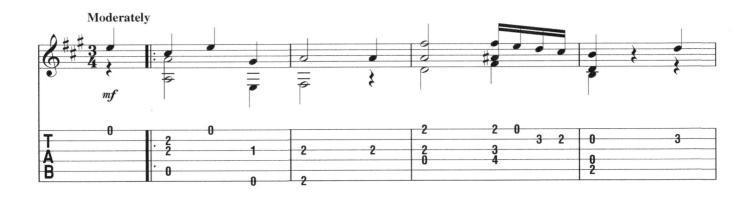

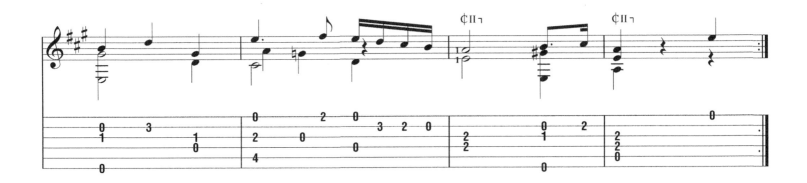

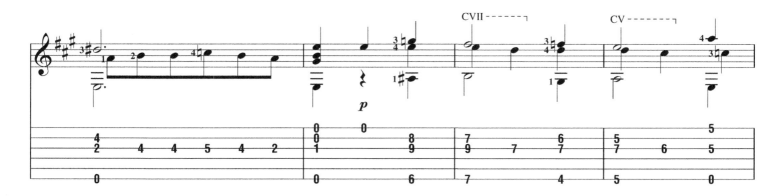

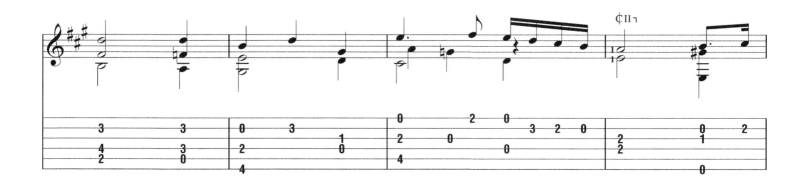

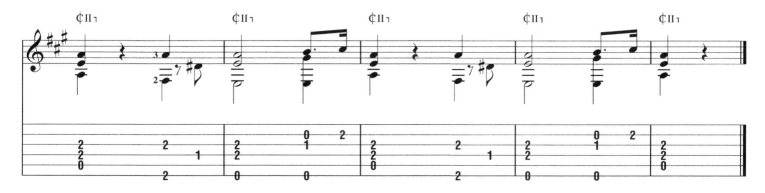

Symphony No. 9 in E Minor

("From the New World")

Second Movement Excerpt

By Antonin Dvořák

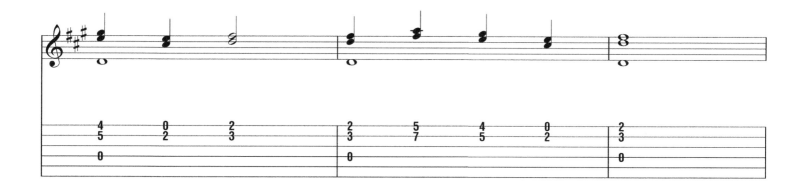

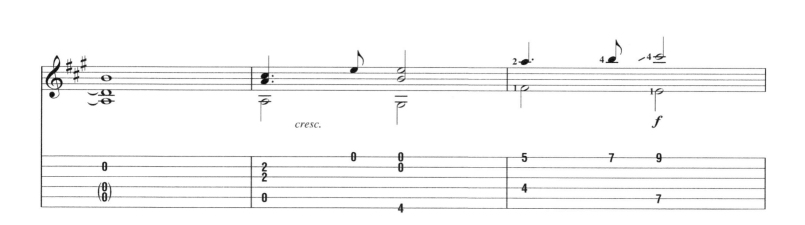

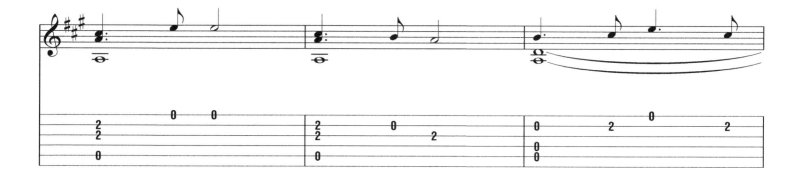

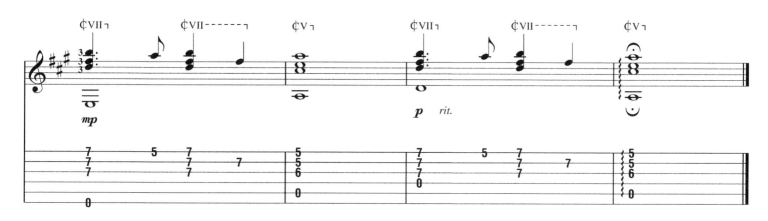

Symphony No. 3

Third Movement Theme

By Johannes Brahms

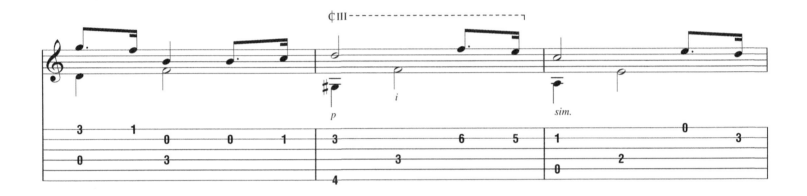

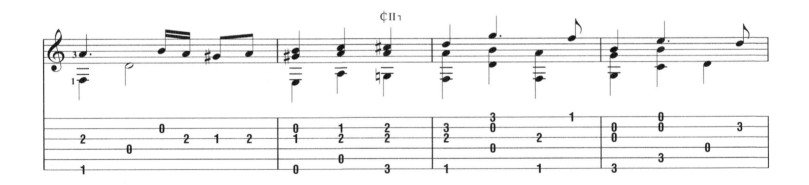

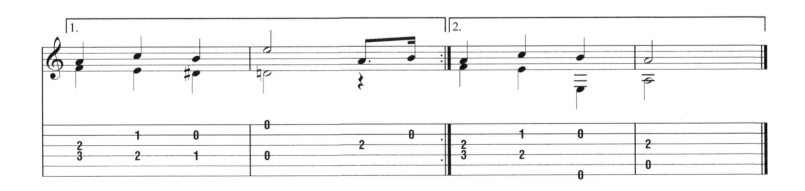

CHERRY LANE
MUSIC COMPANY

6 East 32nd Street, New York, NY 10016

Quality in Printed Music

The Magazine You Can Play

Visit the Guitar One web site at **www.guitarone.com**

ACOUSTIC INSTRUMENTALISTS **INCLUDES TAB**

Over 15 transcriptions from legendary artists such as Leo Kottke, John Fahey, Jorma Kaukonen, Chet Atkins, Adrian Legg, Jeff Beck, and more.

02500399 Play-It-Like-It-Is Guitar............$9.95

THE BEST BASS LINES

24 super songs: Bohemian Rhapsody • Celebrity Skin • Crash Into Me • Crazy Train • Glycerine • Money • November Rain • Smoke on the Water • Sweet Child O' Mine • What Would You Say • You're My Flavor • and more.
02500311 Play-It-Like-It-Is Bass $14.95

BLUES TAB **INCLUDES TAB**

14 songs: Boom Boom • Cold Shot • Hide Away • I Can't Quit You Baby • I'm Your Hoochie Coochie Man • In 2 Deep • It Hurts Me Too • Talk to Your Daughter • The Thrill Is Gone • and more.
02500410 Play-It-Like-It-Is Guitar..........$14.95

CLASSIC ROCK TAB **INCLUDES TAB**

15 rock hits: Cat Scratch Fever • Crazy Train • Day Tripper • Hey Joe • Hot Blooded • Start Me Up • We Will Rock You • You Really Got Me • and more.
02500408 Play-It-Like-It-Is Guitar..........$14.95

MODERN ROCK TAB **INCLUDES TAB**

15 of modern rock's best: Are You Gonna Go My Way • Denial • Hanging by a Moment • I Did It • My Hero • Nobody's Real • Rock the Party (Off the Hook) • Shock the Monkey • Slide • Spit It Out • and more.
02500409 Play-It-Like-It-Is Guitar..........$14.95

SIGNATURE SONGS **INCLUDES TAB**

21 artists' trademark hits: Crazy Train (Ozzy Osbourne) • My Generation (The Who) • Smooth (Santana) • Sunshine of Your Love (Cream) • Walk This Way (Aerosmith) • Welcome to the Jungle (Guns N' Roses) • What Would You Say (Dave Matthews Band) • and more.
02500303 Play-It-Like-It-Is Guitar..........$16.95

BASS SECRETS

WHERE TODAY'S BASS STYLISTS GET TO THE BOTTOM LINE
compiled by John Stix
Bass Secrets brings together 48 columns highlighting specific topics – ranging from the technical to the philosophical – from masters such as Stu Hamm, Randy Coven, Tony Franklin and Billy Sheehan. They cover topics including tapping, walking bass lines, soloing, hand positions, harmonics and more. Clearly illustrated with musical examples.
02500100 ....$12.95

CLASSICS ILLUSTRATED

WHERE BACH MEETS ROCK
by Robert Phillips
Classics Illustrated is designed to demonstrate for readers and players the links between rock and classical music. Each of the 30 columns from *Guitar* highlights one musical concept and provides clear examples in both styles of music. This cool book lets you study moving bass lines over stationary chords in the music of Bach and Guns N' Roses, learn the similarities between "Leyenda" and "Diary of a Madman," and much more!
02500101 ....$9.95

GUITAR SECRETS **INCLUDES TAB**

WHERE ROCK'S GUITAR MASTERS SHARE THEIR TRICKS, TIPS & TECHNIQUES
compiled by John Stix
This unique and informative compilation features 42 columns culled from *Guitar* magazine. Readers will discover dozens of techniques and playing tips, and gain practical advice and words of wisdom from guitar masters.
02500099 ....$10.95

IN THE LISTENING ROOM

WHERE ARTISTS CRITIQUE THE MUSIC OF THEIR PEERS
compiled by John Stix
A compilation of 75 columns from *Guitar* magazine, *In the Listening Room* provides a unique opportunity for readers to hear major recording artists remark on the music of their peers. These artists were given no information about what they would hear, and their comments often tell as much about themselves as they do about the music they listened to. Includes candid critiques by music legends like Aerosmith, Jeff Beck, Jack Bruce, Dimebag Darrell, Buddy Guy, Kirk Hammett, Eric Johnson, John McLaughlin, Dave Navarro, Carlos Santana, Joe Satriani, Stevie Ray Vaughan, and many others.
02500097 ....$14.95

LEGENDS OF LEAD GUITAR

THE BEST OF INTERVIEWS: 1995-2000
This is a fascinating compilation of interviews with today's greatest guitarists! From deeply rooted blues giants to the most fearless pioneers, legendary players reveal how they achieve their extraordinary craft.
02500329 ....$14.95

LESSON LAB

This exceptional book/CD pack features more than 20 in-depth lessons. Tackle in detail a variety of pertinent music- and guitar-related subjects, such as scales, chords, theory, guitar technique, songwriting, and much more!
02500330 Book/CD Pack......................$19.95

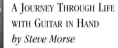

NOISE & FEEDBACK

THE BEST OF 1995-2000: YOUR QUESTIONS ANSWERED
If you ever wanted to know about a specific guitar lick, trick, technique or effect, this book/CD pack is for you! It features over 70 lessons on composing • computer assistance • education and career advice • equipment • technique • terminology and notation • tunings • and more.
02500328 Book/CD Pack......................$17.95

OPEN EARS

A JOURNEY THROUGH LIFE WITH GUITAR IN HAND
by Steve Morse
In this collection of 50 *Guitar* magazine columns from the mid-'90s on, guitarist Steve Morse sets the story straight about what being a working musician *really* means. He deals out practical advice on: playing with the band, songwriting, recording and equipment, and more, through anecdotes of his hard-knock lessons learned.
02500333 ....$10.95

SPOTLIGHT ON STYLE

THE BEST OF 1995-2000: AN EXPLORER'S GUIDE TO GUITAR
This book and CD cover 18 of the world's most popular guitar styles, including: blues guitar • classical guitar • country guitar • funk guitar • jazz guitar • Latin guitar • metal • rockabilly and more!
02500320 Book/CD Pack......................$19.95

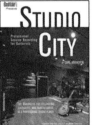

STUDIO CITY

PROFESSIONAL SESSION RECORDING FOR GUITARISTS
by Carl Verheyen
In this collection of columns from Guitar Magazine, guitarists will learn how to: exercise studio etiquette and act professionally • acquire, assemble and set up gear for sessions • use the tricks of the trade to become a studio hero • get repeat call-backs • and more.
02500195 ....$9.95